BIG

Big Maggie

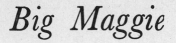

A PLAY IN THREE ACTS BY
JOHN B. KEANE

THE MERCIER PRESS
DUBLIN and CORK

1969 by John B. Keane

Big Maggie is a copyright play and it may not be performed
without a licence.
Applications for licence to perform this play by Amateur Companies
must be made in advance to:
The Mercier Press, Ltd., 4 Bridge Street, Cork
and be accompanied by a fee of £5.25 for each performance.

Professional terms may be had from:
Mr. John B. Keane, William St., Listowel, Co. Kerry, Ireland.

Reprinted 1978

ISBN 0 85342 093 9

Printed by LITHO PRESS CO., MIDLETON

Big Maggie was first produced by Gemini Productions on January 20th 1969 at the Opera House, Cork, with the following cast:

MAGGIE POLPIN	Mary Kean
OLD MAN	Robert Carrickford
OLD WOMAN	Eileen Lemass
GERT	Dearbhla Molloy
BYRNE	Arthur O'Sullivan
MAURICE	Robert Carlile
MICK	Niall O'Brien
KATIE	Liz Davis
TEDDY HEELIN	Gerry Sullivan
MARY MADDEN	Brenda Fricker
MRS MADDEN	Sheila O'Sullivan

Directed by Barry Cassin
Settings by Patrick Murray
Stage Director Mai McFall

CONTENTS

Act One

ACT ONE

Scene One

Action takes place in a graveyard. A near middle-aged woman dressed in black is seated on a headstone buttress smoking a cigarette, with her handbag clutched between her knees.
In the background can be heard the sound of earth falling on a coffin. A man and woman, both old, stop to pay their respects. In turn they shake hands with Maggie Polpin.

OLD MAN Sorry for your trouble, Maggie, he was a good man, God be good to him.

MAGGIE He was so.

OLD WOMAN He was a good man, if he had a failing, Maggie, 'twas a failing many had.

OLD MAN He had a speedy release, God be good to him and that's a lot.

OLD WOMAN Worse if he was after spending six or seven months in a sick bed.

MAGGIE We must be thankful for that! He went quick and that was the way he wanted it. The Lord be good to him!

OLD WOMAN That was a blessing.

OLD MAN *(emphatically)* That was a lot all right. Make no mistake! We can't all go the way we'd like.

MAGGIE We can't.

OLD MAN You may say we can't! There's no one can.

OLD WOMAN He was a cheerful sort of a man.

MAGGIE He was indeed, mam! Cheerful is the word.

OLD MAN What age was he?

MAGGIE He was just turned the sixty.

OLD MAN He didn't get a bad share of it.

OLD WOMAN There's a lot never saw sixty.

OLD MAN And a lot never will! We must be thankful for all things and accept the Holy Will of God.

MAGGIE We must indeed! Well, I won't be holding you up, if you're in a hurry.

OLD MAN I understand, Maggie. You want your own about you at a time like this.

(*Old Man and Old Woman exit and Gert enters*).

GERT Won't you go over to lay on the wreaths?

MAGGIE I won't.

GERT But, mother . . .

MAGGIE Don't but me now, like a good girl. I'm in no humour for it.

GERT I just thought it would be the correct thing to do.

MAGGIE You're not old enough yet to know what is correct and what is not correct. God forgive me if there's two things I can't endure 'tis the likes of them two caterwaulin' about the dead and the other is the thump of clods on a timber coffin. I couldn't bear to watch that gang around the trench and they trying to look sorry. We won't stir from here till they put the last patch on the mound of his grave.

GERT Can I go over to help with the laying of the wreaths?

MAGGIE No! You'll stay here with me. Your brothers and sister can do that. 'Tisn't that the wreaths will do him any good.

GERT Oh, mother, how can you say a thing like that!

MAGGIE It's the truth! God forgive me 'tis a hard thing to say about my own husband, but that's what they'll be saying in the pubs after the funeral. 'Tis what everyone knows. I'm not a trained mourner, Gert. I can't ullagone or moan or look for the arm of another hypocrite to support me.

GERT He was no saint but he was my father. (*rebelliously*) I'm going over to the grave.

MAGGIE *(vehemently)* You will stay where you are, or I'll give you a smack across the puss! I want no more talk out of you now! I have enough to contend with without my youngest wanting to desert me in my hour of need. Listen! The thumping has stopped. They must have the grave half-filled by now. *(thoughtfully)* It won't be long till they thatch it with the green scraws. Call Byrne there! He's on the verge of the crowd.

GERT *(calls in a loud whisper)* Mr Byrne ... Mr Byrne ... *(to Maggie)* He's coming! They're laying down the scraws. Maurice and Mick are doing it. Katie has the wreaths in her arms, she's left do everything!

MAGGIE She's the only one he had any time for! He liked them sonsy and she's all that. I can never be sure but that she isn't fast! *(firmly)* 'Twill be knocked out of her now though! I promise you that.

(Enter Mr Byrne. Easy-going with cap and in the act of putting a pipe into his mouth).

BYRNE Sorry for your trouble, Maggie. You too, miss.

MAGGIE You look it too! Byrne, I want a six foot high limestone monument, three feet across. Three inches thick.

BYRNE 'Tis not customary, Maggie.

MAGGIE What isn't?

BYRNE They generally wait the twelve months before they put up a stone.

MAGGIE Is it *they* will be paying you, or big Maggie Polpin? Oh! I know I'm called Big Maggie and I'm easy!

BYRNE You're the boss, Maggie! When do you want it up?

MAGGIE You can start tomorrow.

BYRNE I don't know that I'll be able to do it tomorrow. I have to start on a Celtic cross for Fonsie MacMee.

MAGGIE How long is Fonsie dead now?

BYRNE Going on the fourteen months. Why?

MAGGIE Well, seeing that he's waited so long, he'll wait a few more days!

BYRNE I don't know, mam! 'Tis commissioned with a bit.

MAGGIE Suit yourself! I'll get someone else to do it if you don't.

BYRNE All right! All right! I'll start tomorrow.

MAGGIE Good! How much will it be? *(opens her purse)*.

BYRNE Well, I can't say off-hand now. There's a lot of things to be taken into consideration.

MAGGIE Six feet by three feet by three inches. You aren't a schoolboy.
(Byrne produces notebook and pencil and starts to do some writing).

BYRNE What's a quarter of eighteen feet?

GERT Four and a half feet.

BYRNE *(writing)* Four and a half feet.

MAGGIE In the honour of God hurry up! 'Tisn't a supermarket we're putting over him!

BYRNE I don't want to wrong you, mam!

MAGGIE You won't, Byrne.

BYRNE *(does a final bit of reckoning)* I can't do it for a penny less than seventy pounds.

MAGGIE Sixty.

BYRNE Can't be done, mam! I don't want to wrong you but I don't want to wrong myself either.

MAGGIE Sixty quid.

BYRNE Sorry!

MAGGIE Cash!

BYRNE Oh, now! . . .

MAGGIE On the nose.

BYRNE Materials is very dear, mam.

MAGGIE Sixty pounds now.

BYRNE All right, I'll take sixty pounds now.
(Maggie hands him the sixty pounds. Byrne counts it carefully).

MAGGIE 'Tis all there, Byrne.

BYRNE I know, but I don't want to wrong you, mam.

MAGGIE The day you wrong me, Byrne, is the day you'll make me pregnant.

BYRNE All the Byrnes, big and small, wouldn't do that, or couldn't do that! We would need softer stone than you, Maggie.

(Gert giggles. In the background is the hum of the rosary. Maggie produces slip of paper).

MAGGIE Here is what you'll inscribe on it. 'Tis all made out.

(Hands him slip of paper. Byrne reads it aloud).

BYRNE WALTER POLPIN. Died March twenty-fifth. Aged sixty-one years. 'Twasn't hard to make out that.

MAGGIE Hard enough, if you were me.

BYRNE No charge for a bit more. Fill it out a bit.

MAGGIE That's the lot! There's no more to be said.

BYRNE Well now, missus, 'tisn't for me to say but they usually say "Erected by his devoted wife and family" or "by his loving wife and family" or some such thing in that line.

MAGGIE Is that a fact! Well, Byrne, there's enough lies written on the headstones of Ireland without my adding to them.

BYRNE I know moderate men that died, Maggie, and they were sorely missed.

MAGGIE I don't doubt it. Will you give me a receipt for my money now, like a good man.

(Byrne shakes his head and makes out a receipt).

Are they finished yet?

GERT Nearly! They're all kneeling around the grave saying a decade.

BYRNE Here's your receipt, mam!

MAGGIE Thank you.

BYRNE *(about to depart)* One last thing, Maggie. Which way do you want it facing?

MAGGIE I'm easy about that, Byrne, so long as it don't face towards me.

(Exit Byrne shaking his head).

GERT You didn't hate him that much!

MAGGIE Didn't I now!

GERT You couldn't hate a person that much!

MAGGIE I never showed it. I couldn't! 'Tis not done you know.

GERT What's going to happen now?

MAGGIE That's none of your business, but I'll tell you this much. The first thing I'm going to do is call a meeting. And this will be the right quare meeting! I'll be the chairman and there won't be any proposing or seconding! I'll be the boss! What I say will go. I have a shop and farm to run and they are going to be run right, or not run at all. If that man that's buried was any damn use, we'd be millionaires.

GERT Oh, come off it, there has to be money!

MAGGIE Has there now!

GERT Well, he was insured for thousands!

MAGGIE You know what, miss? You are getting a bit too forward altogether for my liking. I want no more guff from you. In fact, I won't take any more guff from you!

GERT I didn't mean anything.

MAGGIE You'll turn out like your father if you aren't careful.

GERT That's not fair! I always took your side in everything!

MAGGIE You did, because you had to!

GERT You're terrible!

MAGGIE Why don't you be honest? You know very well he prefered Katie to you!

GERT To you too!

MAGGIE *(slaps her face)* How dare you talk like that to your mother! I could paint a picture of your late, lamented father that would really shock you! I rejected him utterly many years ago when you were a little girl but like all wives, I kept my mind to myself. Pride and ignorance and religion! Those were like chains around me so I stayed put and sang dumb. What's keeping them over there?

GERT I think they're about ready to come.

MAGGIE Wave at them so that they'll know where we are.

(Gert waves).

GERT They see us! They're coming!

MAGGIE *(looks with disapproval about her)* This is one place I won't be buried I can tell you that! I'll fix that shortly too. The earth is a bad enough bed *(indicates cross)* without bedposts like these.

(Enter two young men, dressed in sombre overcoats with black bands around their arms. The older of the two is Maggie's son Maurice. The other is her son Mick).

MAURICE 'Twas a bloody big funeral!

MICK They were there from the city of Limerick!

MAURICE And Tralee.

MICK There was a carload from Cork.

MAURICE A man in a Dublin accent shook hands with me. 'Twas a long way to come for a funeral.

MICK Maybe he was a commercial traveller. He knew a lot of 'em you know.

MAURICE No! I'd say he was a professional man.

MICK Was that the man in the grey coat?

MAURICE Yes! That was him.

MAGGIE Did you fix with the gravediggers?

MAURICE That's all settled.

MAGGIE And the undertaker?

MAURICE Paid in full! Here's the receipt.

(Maggie accepts receipt).

MAGGIE Then we have no more business here. What's keeping the other one?

GERT Here she is now!

(Enter Katie. Attractive girl in a sexy way, dressed in black though she is. She is about twenty-two).

MAGGIE In the honour of God dry your eyes and don't be making a show of yourself!

KATIE I'm entitled to cry when my father is dead.

MAGGIE 'Tis long before this you should have cried for him!

KATIE *(drying her eyes)* Maybe I did.

MAGGIE I can see that you're going to be a problem.

KATIE Is it a sin to cry?

MAGGIE Your bladder is near your eyes, I'm thinking.

MAURICE Talk easy let ye, or we'll be noted!

MAGGIE We're noted long ago! *(to sons)* Maybe the two of you will turn into men now. Long enough you stood back from him!

MAURICE That's not fair!

MAGGIE What about the times he blackguarded me? You were no man you didn't haul out and level him.

MICK He was a big man!

MAGGIE Wasn't there two of you?

MAURICE Let me out of it! I was never a man to come between husband and wife, let alone my father and mother.

MAGGIE You let him abuse me!

MICK You were well able for him! Anyone that abused you wound up second in the long run!

MAGGIE I have a mind to give you a clatter of my handbag!

MICK I wouldn't recommend it.

MAGGIE Wait till I get you home!

MICK It was never a home, ma.

MAGGIE Your father saw to that!

MAURICE Oh, come on for the love of God! We haven't stopped squawking at one another since he died.

18

GERT Maybe now that he's out of the way we might turn into some sort of a family again.

KATIE That's a terrible thing to say!

GERT You were a great one always for closing your eyes at the dirt under your feet!

KATIE I notice a very courageous line of chatter now that he's safely out of the way.

MAGGIE I'm warning you, miss, to hold your tongue! There are a few changes coming shortly that might not altogether appeal to you.

KATIE The king is dead! Long live the king!

MAGGIE That's right. Say your piece now because, believe you me, there's a time coming when you won't have much to say for yourself!

KATIE What are you going to do? Lock me in, is it?

MAGGIE There will be no need for that! You were always used to the good times! We'll see what you're like when the good times are taken away from you.

MAURICE This is a terrible way to be conducting ourselves out here in public.
(Enter old man and woman who sympathized with Maggie and Gert earlier).

MAGGIE Come on away! We can't be wasting our day in idle talk. We have a shop to open.

KATIE You're not going to open the shop today, surely to God!

MAGGIE Why not?

KATIE He's only after being buried!

MAGGIE Not another word out of you madam. Come on, all of you! *(is about to exit).*

OLD MAN Excuse me.

MAGGIE What is it now?

OLD MAN I was wondering if you'd have any notion where Molly Gibbons is buried? There's no stone over her.

MAGGIE I've no idea! Sure isn't one grave as good as

another. 'Tis the thought that counts you know! *(Exit Old Man and Woman).*

A MAN'S VOICE *(off)* Mrs Polpin . . . Mrs Polpin . . .

MAGGIE *(peers in direction of voice)* Who is that? *(All the family turn in direction of voice).*

GERT It's Crawford's traveller.

MAGGIE Young Heelin?

KATIE Yes. Teddy Heelin.

MICK Nice time of the day to show up for a funeral.

KATIE Better late than never.

(Enter Teddy Heelin. He is a young man, extremely good-looking).

TEDDY Terribly sorry I'm late, Mrs Polpin. *(he shakes her hand in sympathy)* Sorry for your trouble.

MAGGIE *(resignedly)* I know that. I know that, boy. 'Twas good of you to come.

TEDDY I had to break a journey. It was only by accident I heard about it. I was on my way to Limerick and I pulled up to get some petrol. The next thing you know the attendant said that Walter Polpin was dead. I hardly believed him. *(takes Katie's hand)* Terribly sorry for your trouble, Katie.

KATIE I know that, Teddy. 'Twas nice of you to come.

TEDDY 'Twas the least I could do.

(Teddy goes and shakes hands with Gert).

TEDDY Sorry Gert.

GERT Thank you, Teddy.

(Teddy shakes hands silently with Mick and Maurice. He then produces a mass card).

TEDDY *(To Maurice)* Will you take this. *(notices that Maurice already has a bundle of same, he hands card to him).*

MAURICE Thanks.

MAGGIE We have to be going. Actually we were just leaving as you arrived.

TEDDY Sorry again, Mrs Polpin. If I'd known I'd have dropped everything to be here on time.

MAGGIE We all know that.

TEDDY If there's anything I can do. Anything. Don't hesitate to ask.

MAURICE We'd better be going.

TEDDY Listen I've got the car outside. I can take some of you down.

GERT (*moves quickly to his side*) I think I'll go with you.

KATIE So will I. That's if you've room for the two of us, Teddy.

TEDDY Oh, there's plenty of room.

MAGGIE No. Katie, you go with your brothers. I'll go with Gert and Mr Heelin. I've a few matters to settle in town, that's if you don't mind waiting a few moments while I look after my affairs, Mr Heelin.

TEDDY I have all day.

MAGGIE That's settled then. Let's get out of this place. (*Exit Teddy holding Gert's arm. They are followed by Maggie*).

MAURICE I'm not sure that I care for that fellow.

KATIE Oh, shut up. You're just jealous of him.

MAURICE You're the one that wanted to go with him.

MICK They say he's a right whoresmaster.

KATIE I wouldn't know about that.

MAURICE Oh come on and let's stop badgering one another for one five minutes. (*Enter Old Man and Woman still searching*).

OLD MAN There's no sign of her anywhere.

OLD WOMAN Maybe 'tisn't here she's buried at all. (*Exit Mick and Maurice*).

MAURICE Are you coming, Katie?

KATIE Coming. (*to Old Man and Old Woman. Points*) Here's our Mr Byrne. He knows all about the graves round here. Ask him and he'll tell you.

OLD MAN Thank you, Miss. We'll do that.

KATIE Don't forget to say a prayer for my father while you're praying for Molly Gibbons.

(Exit Katie).

OLD MAN There's no doubt but he left a mighty strange litter behind him.

OLD WOMAN That last one isn't the worst of them!

OLD MAN Yes! There's a bit of spirit there.

OLD WOMAN Big Maggie Polpin is a dab hand at breaking spirits.

(Enter Byrne).

OLD MAN Good day to you, Mr Byrne!

BYRNE Good day folks!

OLD MAN Fine funeral considering.

BYRNE Yes! Considering.

OLD MAN They say he left her comfortable.

BYRNE Oh, there's no shortage of money. The shop does a good business and that's as good a farm as ever threw up a cow.

OLD WOMAN He was a hard man, God be good to him.

BYRNE *(casually)* There was plenty harder, but they got away with it. He was a man I personally liked. She was wrong for him. She married him for the security.

OLD MAN He was fond of a woman now and again. That's what they say.

BYRNE And by the way you weren't, that's if you ever got the chance!

OLD MAN Who is without a fault, sir?

BYRNE He got his own way always. That's what happened to him. He had the money and he had the appearance and when you have those you get the opportunities. Still I liked him. She was wrong for him. Another woman might have made a better fist of him. 'Tis a mistake to fight fire with fire.

OLD WOMAN They say he drank too.

BYRNE A bottle of whiskey was no bother to him before his breakfast.

OLD MAN Or after it.

OLD WOMAN Whiskey and women. Sure invoices for a coffin.

BYRNE He wasn't the worst of them!

OLD MAN Still you must admit now that he sired a noble share of likely men.

BYRNE Don't I know it! Didn't I see his red hair and big jaw on several here today. Maggie was never able to keep a servant girl in the house you know!

OLD MAN Is that a fact?

BYRNE Oh, that's gospel! There was no stallion the equal of that man if you'll pardon me saying so, missus.

OLD MAN God knows he left a hard woman behind him.

BYRNE She was all right at first. 'Twas the world hardened her. I remember her a handsome girl. She had no real love for him. He was a good catch at the time.

OLD MAN She's no sack of oats now.

BYRNE God bless her she's nicely preserved all right. I won't deny that!

OLD WOMAN What made him turn from a fine woman like that?

BYRNE Wisha, will you tell me, missus, what turns them all? I knew honest men and upright men, sober men and sane men and every one of them was betrayed sooner or later by a rogue of a dickie, if you'll forgive the expression, mam.

OLD WOMAN Oh, God save us! 'Tis a hard plight for an honest man.

BYRNE Did God know what he was doing, mam, or didn't he?

OLD WOMAN God knew.

BYRNE Right you are then! Where does that leave us?

OLD MAN As wise as ever! I do often say to myself, why

people do be so slow to kiss goodbye to this goddamn world of pains and aches and puking. Eh!

OLD WOMAN Robbery and hypocrisy and murder from one end of the day to the other.

OLD MAN Life is the grimmest loan of all, my friend. The interest is too high in the end.

OLD WOMAN 'Tis the cross of man, life is.

BYRNE You'll be thankful to be leaving it so.

OLD MAN Listen here to me.

BYRNE Yes?

OLD MAN Would you by any chance know where the grave of Molly Gibbons is?

BYRNE Which Molly Gibbons now? Was it the Molly Gibbons that was tackled to Donal Summers or was it the Molly Gibbons that was housekeeper for Canon Mackintosh the Protestant?

OLD MAN 'Twas the canon's housekeeper.

BYRNE (thoughtfully) Molly Gibbons that worked for Canon Mackintosh. Well, now. (points with finger) Down there at the left hand corner you'll notice a wild rose bush. There's a cypress 'longside of it. Molly is wedged between the two.

OLD WOMAN We're thankful to you.

BYRNE For nothing mam!

OLD MAN We promised a prayer first for the man they just put under. I fancy he won't be getting many.

BYRNE Well now. I do be here most of the day and you could count on one hand the number that comes to pray. But the man that went under now has no more prayers to get, and from the cut of the widow, I'd say she won't think of the next world till she enters it.

OLD MAN So long so!

OLD WOMAN Good luck to you sir!

BYRNE Good day to you both!

(Exit Old Man and Old woman).

(produces his pipe) Limestone. Six feet by three feet by

three inches. 'Tis a respectable block of stone. 'Twill be there when he's forgotten and 'twill be there when he's rotten, and may God have mercy on the poor man's immortal soul!

CURTAIN
for end of Scene I, Act I

ACT ONE

Scene Two

Action takes place that night in the sitting room of the house of Maggie Polpin.

GERT I'm dying to hear all.

MAURICE I wish I could be so cheerful.

MICK I suppose she's going to tell us now.

MAURICE She can't keep us waiting much longer.
   (Katie enters carrying cash box).

KATIE She's coming now.

MAURICE Be quiet the lot of you.
   (Maggie enters).

MAGGIE You can compose yourselves awhile, but I'm going to advise you all, to be ready for changes. *(lights a cigarette)*.

GERT Can I have one?

MAGGIE No.

GERT Ah please, mother.

MAGGIE No! When I say no, I mean it.

GERT If you said no to a fellow you liked, would you mean it?

MAURICE We're turning into a rough family.

KATIE Ah, shut up you.

MICK Is it fair to ask if there was a will?

MAGGIE You'll know all in a minute. Keep your shirt on. *(to Maurice)* Sit down. *(to Katie)* Shop locked?

KATIE Yes.

MAGGIE Did you pay the workmen?

KATIE They're paid.

MAGGIE Is all the cash here? *(indicates cashbox)*.

KATIE Yes.

MAGGIE And all the receipts?

KATIE What's the matter? Don't you trust me?

MAGGIE I trust no one.

KATIE Do you mean I'm dishonest?

MAGGIE I never met anyone who admitted to being dishonest so I wouldn't know about those things. Now let you all listen carefully to what I have to say. It concerns each of you. You asked a while ago, Mick, if there was a will. Well, there wasn't.

KATIE Impossible!

MAGGIE There was no will.

KATIE (desperately) But there has to be a will! He always promised me.

MAGGIE Promised you what?

KATIE Nothing.

MAGGIE More than me maybe?

KATIE I didn't say that.

MAGGIE Now, there being no will, as I said, that puts me in charge, which is only as it should be.

MICK If there's no will how can it all be yours? We're all entitled to our share.

MAGGIE There's no will because a year ago your father signed over the place to me.

KATIE What!

MICK I don't believe you.

MAGGIE Don't you now. Ring up the solicitor and see what he has to say.

MICK You're bluffing.

MAGGIE The phone is in the shop, lift it. If you don't believe me you'll believe D'Arcy the solicitor.

KATIE Sure how could my father do a thing like that, he promised.

MAGGIE Do I tell lies? Do I? . . . Well come on, you've known me long enough and you're quick enough to criticise . . . well, speak up one of you . . . am I a liar?

MAURICE No.

MAGGIE Anyway why would I waste my time telling a silly lie like that when a phone call from one of you would make a fool of me?

GERT I believe you.

MAGGIE So you should. Here it is now – this time a year ago I had a talk with your father and he agreed to sign over the place to me. He had good reason to.

KATIE Did you blackmail him?

MAGGIE You'll learn to bite that tongue of yours miss, when I have a minute to deal with you – and that might be sooner than you think.

KATIE I asked you a question.

MAGGIE And you'll get an answer. I got no more than my rights. I brought a thousand pounds fortune when I came here, and I've slaved here for twenty-five years. I don't think anyone here will deny that. *(to Katie)* Unless you would like to put your spoke in.

KATIE I've nothing to say.

MAGGIE Good. Now do any of you still feel like making that phone call.

MICK All right. Tell us how much he left anyway.

MAGGIE Death duties, that's what he left – enough to keep me struggling for years to come.

MAURICE Well, tell us how we stand.

MAGGIE I don't understand you.

MAURICE What are we going to get out of it?

MAGGIE You'll get nothing out of it naturally, not yet anyway. You have a roof over your heads. You have good food and you'll have pocket money.

MICK *(scornfully)* Pocket money! You're mad if you think I'm going to stay here for pocket money. Pocket money is for kids. If I'm to stay here I'll want a share. It was all understood that the farm would be divided between myself and Maurice.

MAGGIE Understood by whom? It wasn't understood by me. Who told you all this?

MICK You had better get it clear, mother. I am not going
to be a servant boy any longer. If the farm isn't divided
immediately and by divided, I mean that both halves
will be fully stocked with cattle, machinery and
working capital together with dwelling house and
outhouses.

MAGGIE Obviously you've been talking to someone!
You'd never think up all that by yourself!

MICK Well, are you or aren't you?

MAGGIE Am I or aren't I what?

MICK Going to divide the farm?

MAGGIE I'll have to see.

MICK You'll see right now! I am not going to be fobbed
off by promises.

MAGGIE Mick, I'm in no position to guarantee anything
to anybody.

MICK In that case you can look for someone else to run
the farm. I'm resigning. Are you coming, Maurice?
(No reply from Maurice).

MICK I'm going, Mother.

MAGGIE Well, you know how to turn the knob on the
door, boy, and you can take it from me that no one
here is going to call you back.

MICK Are you coming, Maurice?
(Maurice does not reply).

KATIE Maurice, you were spoken to.

MICK Are you coming, Maurice, for the last time?
(Maurice does not reply).

MAGGIE He won't go! He hasn't the guts of a louse!

MICK Maurice?

MAURICE I'm saying nothing. I've had enough squabb-
ling for one day.

MAGGIE True to form.

MICK I'll need money. Not much and permission to stay
the night. I can't go anywhere till morning.

MAGGIE Yes, a good night's sleep is important.

30

MICK Damn you!

MAGGIE Off to bed now, like a good boy.

MICK My father is a lucky man to be freed of you. I'm beginning to have sympathy for him now.

(Exit Mick).

MAGGIE He'll change his mind. He knows where his rations come from. Have you anything to say, Maurice?

MAURICE *(stands up)* Yes I have!

MAGGIE No time like the present. Out with it!

MAURICE I want to get married.

MAGGIE You do?

MAURICE Yes I do!

MAGGIE And do I know the lady of your choice?

GERT I know her. She's Mary Madden from Knock-liney.

MAGGIE Dan Madden's daughter?

MAURICE Yes.

MAGGIE Sit down boy.

(Maurice sits).

What has Dan Madden? Fifteen or sixteen cows is it?

MAURICE Yes.

MAGGIE And seven or eight other young children to be provided for?

MAURICE Yes. You have your facts.

MAGGIE And where do you expect to live?

MAURICE Why? Here of course! Where else would I go?

MAGGIE Where else indeed?

MAURICE Then it's all right?

MAGGIE Do you know how much money I had when I came as mistress to this house?

MAURICE You told us. You had a thousand pounds.

MAGGIE And how much has this Madden one?

MAURICE She hasn't anything.

MAGGIE And you expect me to hand over the reins after my twenty-five years to a slip of a girl without a brown penny in her pocket?

MAURICE Well, no.

MAGGIE Then what do you expect?

MAURICE We could live here with you. A temporary thing, and I could work away on the farm for my wages until . . . well until.

MAGGIE Until I kick the bucket! Isn't that it?

MAURICE It's not! All I want is to get married. There's nothing exorbitant about that.

MAGGIE Well, you tell her to find a fortune of fifteen hundred quid and I'll consider her proposal.

MAURICE But she hasn't that kind of money and neither have I. At that rate I'll be waiting for ever to get married.

MAGGIE Go on and marry for love so.

MAURICE I have no money.

MAGGIE But if you marry for love you don't need money.

MAURICE So you say.

MAGGIE You're only twenty-four. Your father was thirty-five when he married and there were people who considered him young.

MAURICE God Almighty Mother, give me a break! I'm in love with the girl. She's a good girl! You'll like her!

MAGGIE I'd like her a lot better if she had fifteen hundred pounds.

MAURICE But what am I going to do?

MAGGIE Forget it for the present is my advice. We'll talk about it some other time.

MAURICE Will you consider it some other time?

(Knock at door).

GERT I'll go.

MAGGIE Stay where you are.

MAURICE Will you consider it? Please, Mother.

MAGGIE We'll see, we'll see. Now don't think about it any more for a while and we'll see what the future holds.

(Knock at door. Maggie exits).

MAURICE Do you believe her?

GERT I believe her – if Mary Madden can't put down the cash my mother won't let her darken the door.

MAURICE No – I mean about the will.

GERT Sure she said it would be easy to catch her out. Oh I believe her all right. She told me once that the worst thing about telling lies isn't that it's a sin, but it's such a waste of time trying to wriggle out of it when you're found out.

MAURICE My father promised me the farm.

GERT Mick said it was to be divided.

MAURICE 'Twas promised to me.

KATIE Is that why you sang dumb when Mick asked you to go away with him – so you could have it all to yourself?

MAURICE Mick can make up his own mind, it's nothing to do with me.

GERT He's your brother isn't he? Are you going to –

MAURICE We've had enough fighting for one day. It's best if we all mind our own affairs.

KATIE Well you're a cool one I'll say that for you. But you haven't a hope in hell of getting married unless my mother can jingle out the wedding march with the Madden's fifteen hundred quid.

MAURICE Oh lay off. Now that the old fellow's dead there'll be a quick stop to your gallop. This time last year you got everything your own way, the rest of us mightn't have been around for all he cared.

GERT Stop it the pair of you, this is getting us no place.

KATIE Where's there to get. Give us a fag someone.

MAURICE Here. Why in God's name did he have to sign everything over to her!

GERT A year ago. And he never let on.

KATIE A year ago. Moll Sonders.

MAURICE What about her.

KATIE You remember the time she caught him with Moll?

GERT I don't believe that. I don't believe he ever had anything to do with Moll Sonders.

MAURICE Now that I come to think of it Moll stopped coming here about a year before he died.

KATIE You remember our beloved mother was supposed to go to see that doctor in Dublin?
(*Others nod*).
She left here in a hired car at eight o'clock. She was to stay over-night. You two and Mick had gone into town to a dance. I went to bed early that night because I was out the night before.

MAURICE I remember.

KATIE She didn't go to Dublin at all. She got the driver to turn round after dark and came straight back here. If I had known I could have tipped my father off.

GERT (*shocked*) You knew Moll was with him?

KATIE I know she had called to see him just after I went to bed but I knew nothing else. It could have been for anything. It could have been for a loan of money. You all know he couldn't say no. Besides her husband was in England and he wasn't sending her anything.

GERT You'd swear black and white to save him.

KATIE I would and what about it! He was a man what none of you are.

MAURICE Oh, cut it out and get on with the story.

KATIE Moll arrived about ten o'clock. They spoke in whispers but I knew who it was. About twenty minutes after Moll's arrival I heard someone tiptoeing past my door and going on up the stairs to my father's room.

MAURICE My mother!

KATIE I opened my door and peeped out and I saw the back of her just outside my father's door. I nearly dropped dead. There was nothing I could do. She burst in the door and caught him red-handed.

MAURICE . . . Can you be sure?

KATIE Look! I saw Moll Sonders running down the stairs in her birthday suit and my mother after her. Is that enough for you?

GERT He was nothing but an animal.

KATIE Oh shut up. I didn't blame him.

MAURICE My God, you're as bad as him.

KATIE For the love of God. My mother didn't sleep with him for years and when she did I doubt if she was any good to him.

MAURICE Here now, I'm not going to let you talk like that.

KATIE Oh, grow up! I was at Cloonlara Races with him once and he was in the bar swapping yarns with a crowd of his cronies. They were talking about their wives. I remember him to say that he was married for eighteen years and he never once saw his wife naked!

GERT You can't talk like that. It's terrible. Stop her. Maurice.

KATIE The bother with you is that you never tried to understand my father. All those men in the bar that night had the same story. They didn't know I was listening. The wives were too damn good. Damn them, they thought it was a sacrilege to fornicate with their own husbands.

MAURICE I've given you up long ago but I never dreamed a girl of your upbringing, educated by the nuns, could even think like that, not to mind talk. You're past understanding.

KATIE Maybe I am but I'm not deaf and I am not blind

35

to what's happening about me like the two of you are.

GERT I'm not going to listen to any more of this.

KATIE Suit yourself.

MAURICE Was that what led to his signing over everything to her?

KATIE Of course it was. I know that he went on an awful booze after that and he spent weeks without leaving his room after that again.

MAURICE I remember that and I remember D'Arcy the solicitor called and went upstairs with Byrne and my mother.

KATIE That's it. Byrne was the witness. She got it all done while most of us were out. She has us where she wants us now. Here she comes.

MAGGIE *(entering)* Nellie Riordan at the door dragging three kids and a pram full of potatoes. Came to pay her respects. She'd pray for the deceased and say the stations – which would take her a lot less time than she kept me at the door. Well there's no need to ask what you were talking about, but I can tell you that your conversation was as big a waste of time as mine was with Nellie.

MAURICE Look, Mother, I'll go up and see if I can talk some sense into Mick.

MAGGIE Yes, do that.

MAURICE And you'll definitely consider what I asked you another time.

MAGGIE Trust me, Maurice. For years before he died your father drank and spent most of what we made here. It couldn't go on, I had to stop it. Now I know you understand so don't press me for details. We'll work hard now and get the place going again. Go along now, God is good.
(Exit Maurice).

KATIE You haven't an earthly notion of letting him

marry that girl. Why didn't you tell him the truth?

MAGGIE He'll get over her. Besides he's a good worker and help is hard to get. There's plenty of time for him to marry.

KATIE Jesus, you're a hard case!

MAGGIE How dare you take the Holy Name in my presence!

KATIE 'Twas from you I picked it up.

MAGGIE I'll let that ball over the bar for the present. You're your father's daughter all right! Just try to remember there's new management here now.

KATIE Don't I know it!

MAGGIE I'll tell you about the arrangements I have for you shortly. It might drive some of the steam out of your engine.

KATIE I can't wait!

MAGGIE Believe you me, you'll be sorry you said that.

KATIE Free country you know.

MAGGIE Shut up you rip or I'll strike you. *(to Gert)* Gert, you are to leave the kitchen and come into the shop with me, unless you want to get married too.

GERT Oh no! I'd see more of Crawford's traveller in the shop, wouldn't I?

MAGGIE You like him?

GERT He's a lamb.

MAGGIE He's a good-looking scoundrel all right. I'll say that for him. You can talk away to him in the shop but otherwise you are to have nothing to do with him, do you hear?

GERT I hear.

MAGGIE Good.

KATIE I'd like to ask a question.

MAGGIE Go ahead.

KATIE If Gert is to go into the shop and if you and I are already in the shop, who is going to do the kitchen?

37

MAGGIE Can't you compose yourself! Amn't I coming to that. You think I make these arrangements on the spur of the moment.

KATIE We don't want three of us in the shop.

MAGGIE I couldn't agree with you more, so I've decided that you are to do the kitchen.

KATIE Not a hope!

MAGGIE You'll do the kitchen, Gert deserves a turn in the shop.

KATIE I won't do the kitchen!

MAGGIE Now listen to me. I have no intention of making a game out of it. We're both too old for this "I will" and "I won't" business. From tomorrow morning, you will begin work in the kitchen. If you don't, I'll send you out of this house a pauper. How would you like that?

KATIE I could always make a living.

MAGGIE *(meaningfully)* I'm afraid you could.

KATIE Oh, by God, now we're getting the innuendos. Could you tender an addition to that implication?

MAGGIE Will you take it now, or will you wait till you get it?

(Enter Mick wearing his overcoat).

I must say you weren't long coming back.

(But Mick ignores her and goes directly to where the cashbox is. He is about to take it up in his hands when Maggie intervenes).

Here! What in hell do you think you're doing?

MICK I need a few pounds. It's my due.

KATIE Don't leave, Mick! Don't give in to her. 'Tis what she wants.

MAGGIE *(to Katie)* Keep out of this.

(Mick snatches the cashbox from under Maggie's hand. He opens it and looks inside).

MICK *(to Katie)* How much is in here; a hundred? A hundred and twenty?

KATIE There's ninety-seven pounds in cash.

MAGGIE Don't touch that money.

MICK *(to Maggie)* Keep back or I'll give you a belt. I swear to God I will!
(He takes the money from the cashbox and puts it in his pocket).

MAGGIE If you don't put back that money this instant you will never darken the door of this house again.

MICK Don't worry, you'll hear no more from me.

MAGGIE I mean it.

MICK And I mean it.

MAGGIE You're finished with this place. Remember that!

MICK *(to Katie)* I'll want the loan of your car to take me to the station. You can collect it in the morning.

KATIE You're welcome. The keys are in it. Good luck darling!

MICK Goodbye Katie. Goodbye Gert.
(They mumble embarrassed goodbyes).
(Exit Mick).

GERT *(a little appalled)* Is he gone for ever?

MAGGIE Never mind him for the present. *(to Katie)* Now you see the trouble my family is causing me. You can forget about your car too if the kitchen doesn't suit you.

KATIE It's my car.

MAGGIE Who pays the tax and insurance and who buys the petrol? It's the property of the house.

KATIE You wouldn't take away my car!

MAGGIE My car if you don't go into the kitchen. The kitchen will do you good. I have big plans for you!

KATIE Get one thing into your head right now, my mother. You will not dominate me.

MAGGIE Of course you know what you can do, don't you?

KATIE What is that?

MAGGIE You can blow any time you want! If you won't

do what you're told I don't want you around.

KATIE I suppose I could get a job in a shop.

MAGGIE No! Not you! You're too used to a good time, too used to having a car under your behind.

KATIE All right. I'll call your bluff. I'll start in the kitchen tomorrow morning. Anything else?

MAGGIE Be sure there is. There's a lot more. *(to Gert)* You go out to the kitchen and put on a fry for me and see that you don't burn the rashers like you did this morning! Hurry up! *(to Katie)* I'm not finished with you! Our little conference is only beginning. *(to Gert)* Move!

(Exit Gert. Maggie rises to make sure that nobody is listening from the outside. She returns to her seat with a key in her hand, having locked the door).

MAGGIE First things first. Did Johnny Conlon propose to you a year ago?

KATIE He did!

MAGGIE Is he still to the good?

KATIE He is.

MAGGIE Is he still interested?

KATIE He is, but I'm not.

MAGGIE Why didn't you tell me the time he proposed to you?

KATIE It wasn't important and besides I turned him down. He's not my type.

MAGGIE You'll marry him and you'll marry him within the next three months which is more.

KATIE You're a howl!

MAGGIE You'll marry him!

(Katie laughs).

Laugh while you can.

KATIE I laughed before this you know.

MAGGIE You're twenty-two years of age and you haven't a penny to your name without my say so.

(Katie still laughs).

MAGGIE *(calmly)* You'll marry him.

KATIE *(getting over laughter)* I told you before he's not my type.

(Maggie rises again and goes to exit to make sure she is not being heard).

MAGGIE *(coldly)* What is your type?

KATIE *(uncomfortably)* Well not him anyway.

MAGGIE Would you like me to tell you?

KATIE I don't know what you mean.

MAGGIE I think you do, Katie!

KATIE This is worse than a courtroom.

MAGGIE The night of the creamery social, you went to the dance with Gert.

KATIE So did three or four hundred other girls.

MAGGIE We'll forget about those! It's you and Gert that concern me. You sat with Gert throughout the dinner but after the dinner you went to the Public bar.

KATIE I did! But if you already know all this, why do you need to ask me?

MAGGIE *(white with temper locates a sweeping brush)* You see this brush?

KATIE *(losing some of her assurance)* I do.

MAGGIE Well, listen to me, Katie. As sure as your father is in his grave tonight, I'll break this brush across your back if you give me another single word of back-chat.

KATIE *(afraid)* Yes, Mother.

MAGGIE Now, you went to the public bar?

KATIE Yes, Mother.

MAGGIE With whom did you go, Katie?

KATIE Gert told you.

MAGGIE Gert did not tell me. Gert doesn't know. Now, with whom did you go to the bar!

KATIE Let me alone, can't you. I'm all torn up after the funeral and I can't take any more of it.

MAGGIE All right, you went to the bar. I don't mind

that. But tell me the name of the man who was with you?

KATIE What man?

MAGGIE *(angrily)* His name!

KATIE Toss Melch.

MAGGIE So it was Toss Melch.

KATIE Yes.

MAGGIE Was his wife with him?

KATIE No.

MAGGIE Where did you first meet him?

KATIE Last year at another social.

MAGGIE So you've known him a year?

KATIE Yes.

MAGGIE And before the night of the creamery social, how many times did you meet him?

KATIE Four or five times.

MAGGIE In the bar, the night of the creamery social, how many drinks had you?

KATIE Just a few. Two or three. I forget exactly.

MAGGIE You had six halves of gin.

KATIE *(really afraid)* Yes. Yes.

MAGGIE I've known all this for a while but with your father around I was powerless to do anything. Now at half past eleven, this married man Toss Melch booked a room in the hotel and he went upstairs immediately. When he left, what did you do?

KATIE I had a dance or two.

MAGGIE And after that?

KATIE Well, I went upstairs. But it was only to go to the ladies' cloakroom.

MAGGIE But there is a ladies' cloakroom downstairs.

KATIE It was crowded. Mobbed. I tried to get in a few times but it was next to impossible.

MAGGIE And how long were you in the upstairs ladies' cloakroom?

KATIE *(convincingly)* It was before twelve when I came

42

down. I'm sure of that.

MAGGIE No, it wasn't! You came downstairs at five minutes to two just before the social ended.

KATIE *(fearfully)* It's a lie! *(buries her head in her hands)* It's a lie!

MAGGIE It's not a lie! You went upstairs at quarter to twelve and you didn't come down till five minutes to two. Don't deny it! Now what were you doing upstairs for nearly two and a quarter hours?

KATIE Nothing. I was doing nothing, Mother.

MAGGIE Katie, you were seen. Two days after that night I had an anonymous letter from someone who signed herself a friend. *(viciously)* Tell me what you were doing upstairs?

KATIE Nothing. Nothing I tell you!

MAGGIE *(advancing upon her and seizing her by the hair of the head. Swings Katie around so that she faces her)* You went into the room booked by Melch and you stayed there with him for two and a quarter hours. What were you doing? *(Katie is silent; Maggie slaps her face)* Have I raised a whore? *(screams)* Have I raised a whore? Have I? *(still holding her by the hair she shakes her)* Tell me what you were doing in that room or I'll beat you so that your own sister won't know you. *(Lifts her by hair off chair and still holding her hair she forces her to kneel on floor).*

KATIE *(weakly)* Oh God help me!

MAGGIE I'll help you, you doxie! You tart! Tell me now before I lose control of myself! What were you doing in that room with Toss Melch? *(screams)* Tell me!

KATIE *(weakly)* I was committing a sin.

MAGGIE Louder! I can't hear you!

KATIE I was committing a sin with him.

MAGGIE And it wasn't your first time?

KATIE No. No. I couldn't help myself.

MAGGIE *(letting go of her hair)* Get up!

(Katie is still kneeling and sobbing).
Get up off your knees and act like a woman.
(Katie rises slowly).

KATIE Sure you won't beat me?

MAGGIE No! I won't beat you. I was mistaken about you! I thought you were more brazen, more of a woman. You're still a child!
(Maggie lights herself a cigarette)
(tendering cigarette) You want one of these?
(Trembling, Katie snatches it. Maggie lights it for her).
Sit.
(Katie sits immediately).

KATIE What are you going to do to me?

MAGGIE Why should I do anything to you when you've already disgraced yourself.

KATIE Will I be left stay here?

MAGGIE You will; under certain conditions.

KATIE I agree, Mother.
(Maggie locates writing pad and pen).

MAGGIE Since Johnny Conlon proposed to you has he been in touch with you at all?

KATIE He has tried. He salutes always and he wrote a few times.

MAGGIE Here's some notepaper. Write back to him. Tell him you would like if he called, that you are down and out after the death of your father and whatever else occurs to you.
(Maggie goes towards exit).
Bring me the letter before you put it in the envelope.
If we play our cards properly he may propose to you again. I'm going to the kitchen. Tell him from me, thanks for his mass card, that I appreciate the thought. Will you tell him that, Katie?

KATIE Yes.

MAGGIE First thing in the morning, before I forget it, get into town and collect your car.

KATIE Are you going somewhere?

MAGGIE No, I'm not going anywhere, but it just occurred to me that it's about time I learned how to drive.

CURTAIN
for end of Act I.

Act Two

ACT TWO

Scene One

*Action takes place in the shop of Maggie Polpin. It is a
country shop where almost everything is sold.*
The time is three months later, mid-morning.
*Mr Byrne is at the counter with a message bag in his hand.
Behind the counter is Gert. She is adding items on a piece of
paper. Says half to herself, half to Byrne:*

GERT Pound of butter, bread, washing soap, toilet soap,
sugar, tea, bacon, tobacco . . . Did I give you the
tobacco?

BYRNE You did! I have it here in my pocket. Are you
all right, Gert?

GERT I am . . . thanks.

BYRNE Are you sure?

GERT *(a trifle impatiently)* Thanks. I can handle her. I
know I can.

BYRNE I hope so.

GERT That's the lot so. Will you keep an eye here for a
few minutes till I check these prices with my mother?

BYRNE Fire away, but don't be all day. I've work to do.
Tell your mother I was asking for her.

GERT I will. I won't be a jiff!
*(Exit Gert. Byrne locates his pipe and lights it. Enter Teddy
Heelin).*

TEDDY Good morning!

BYRNE Not a bad morning.

TEDDY Not bad. It's nice outside. Seems to be clearing.

BYRNE You're with Crawfords, aren't you?

TEDDY That's right. I had no idea I was so well-known.

BYRNE How are things around the country?

TEDDY Things could be better but then again they were often worse. Anybody around?

BYRNE Gert will be out in a minute. Just went in to check a few prices with her mother. I suppose you meet all kinds in your travels?

TEDDY All kinds. Believe you me my friend. All kinds.

BYRNE I can imagine.

TEDDY Oh, you'd be amazed.

BYRNE Travelling is a job I wouldn't like.

TEDDY You never know till you've tried.

BYRNE I daresay that's true.

TEDDY Is Gert in the shop now?

BYRNE Oh yes! For the past few months, since the father died.

TEDDY He went quick, didn't he?

BYRNE Sudden. The heart.

TEDDY Sudden is the best way.

BYRNE So they say.

TEDDY The oldest girl Katie. Where is *she*?

BYRNE Married.

TEDDY You're not serious.

BYRNE Fortnight ago. Fellow a few miles down the road, big farmer.

TEDDY God knows 'tis hard to believe. I thought she'd knock a few more berls out of the world before she dropped anchor.

BYRNE 'Twas a surprise all right.

TEDDY She was a gay woman.

BYRNE Gay?

(They laugh).

The young fellow is gone too, Mick.

TEDDY I met him at the funeral. He worked on the farm, didn't he?

BYRNE That's right.

TEDDY Where did he go?

BYRNE Don't know.

TEDDY What happened?

BYRNE Fell out with the mother.

TEDDY Oh! How's she since Polpin died?

BYRNE Bearing up well, mind you.

TEDDY What's Katie's husband like?

BYRNE Very nice man. Very well off. Bit advanced of course. Would want to get his gun oiled I'd say. You'd be a likelier man now for taking a crack at a target like Katie.

TEDDY And how do you know that I didn't score a few bulls-eyes there before this?

BYRNE It 'twouldn't surprise me! It wouldn't surprise me one bit, my friend. Here's Gert.
(Enter Gert still checking list of messages. When she notices Teddy Heelin she shows her delight).

GERT Teddy Heelin! How are you? *(shakes his hand).*

TEDDY Couldn't be better thanks be to God. How're you!

GERT Fine! Fine! I'll be with you in a minute, Teddy, as soon as I finish here. *(to Byrne)* The whole thing comes to two pounds one.

BYRNE *(locating money)* Two pounds one. Here you are. *(Gert accepts money and deposits it in cash register).*
Did you tell her I was asking for her?

GERT Who!

BYRNE Your mother!

GERT I did!

BYRNE What did she say?

GERT She laughed.

BYRNE What kind of a laugh was it?

GERT How do you mean?

BYRNE Well, was it a short laugh or a long laugh. Was it a wicked laugh or a gay laugh?

GERT She seemed to enjoy it.

BYRNE Good. Very good!

TEDDY How's business, Gert?

GERT Not bad. She has a big order for you.

TEDDY Good! That's what we like to hear.

GERT He's a right charmer, Mr Byrne. He gets orders everywhere.

BYRNE I wouldn't doubt it!

TEDDY 'Tis the quality of the goods, not me, Mr Byrne!

GERT Oh, go on out o' that! Everyone knows he's a ladies' man! They say he has more sex appeal than any other two travellers.

BYRNE That's no bad mark against him. I could use a bit of it myself.

GERT When are you going to take me out to dinner, Teddy Heelin?

TEDDY Do you want your mother to horsewhip me?

GERT Oh, she lets me out now. I can go wherever I like and with whom. She knows I'm sensible.

TEDDY If you're serious, I'll take you out some night.

GERT I'm serious. It was always Katie he noticed before, Mr Byrne. He used to call me the baby.

BYRNE She's no baby now my friend, but by God she has the equipment to feed one.

GERT Mr Byrne!

TEDDY I won't disagree with you there. The reason I always noticed Katie was that she was in the shop and you were in the kitchen but if you want the truth, you were the one I was interested in and I'll prove it to you now by taking you out any night you care to name.

BYRNE That's fair enough!

GERT Mr Byrne, didn't I hear you saying a while ago that you had work to do?

BYRNE I get the message! I won't stand in the way of romance. *(is about to exit)* But I'll tell the two of you this for your own good. Don't be too hasty to say anything to Maggie. She'll be slower than a parish priest to give a blessing to what doesn't suit her.
(Exit Byrne).

GERT Don't take any notice of him. He's nice really!

TEDDY Are you serious about my taking you out?

GERT I am!

TEDDY I'd have asked you for a date long before this, but I didn't want to cross your mother.

GERT Are you afraid of her too?

TEDDY Being afraid of her has nothing to do with it. She's one of my best customers and I don't want to fall out with her. When you're a commercial traveller, you have to be cautious. You don't make demands. You take what you get. *(leans across counter and takes Gert's hands)* What time do you want me to call tonight?

GERT What time would suit you?

TEDDY After the post goes out I'm free. I could call any time after that.

GERT Half seven be all right?

TEDDY I'll be here. Your mother won't mind?

GERT No! She likes you. In fact she said so. Oh, she says you're a bit of a playboy and that you'd want watching. But she does like you.

TEDDY Where do you want to go tonight?

GERT I don't mind.

TEDDY We can decide that when I call.

GERT You won't get fresh with me now. I wouldn't like that! I'm not that kind. You had better know in time.

TEDDY I know you're not. That's why I'm so keen to take you out.

GERT The novelty I suppose.

TEDDY No! I think about you in a very special way. I wouldn't want to do anything to hurt you.

GERT I believe you.

(Teddy takes her face in his hands and kisses her).

(not unkindly) Stop it you eejit! Do you want someone to walk in!

TEDDY I'm no saint! But I suppose you know that.

GERT I've heard things.

53

TEDDY You don't have to worry. I wouldn't harm a hair of your head. I just want to be near you. *(kisses her)* To hear you talking, laughing, whispering!

GERT *(laughs)* Whispering?

TEDDY Yes! Whispering! Something tells me that you're a terrific whisperer and if there's one thing I love it's to hear a nice girl whispering!

GERT You're a scream!

TEDDY Whisper something to me now!

GERT *(indulging him)* What will I whisper to you?

TEDDY Anything you like.

GERT All right then. *(She whispers into his ear).*

TEDDY *(upon hearing it he draws away)* I'm shocked. I'm scandalized! How could you say such a thing!

GERT But all I said was it's a nice day.

TEDDY That's it! It's not just a nice day! It's a lovely day! It's a beautiful day, or do you know the day we have?

GERT I do! It's Tuesday!

TEDDY *(shakes his head)* NO! No! No! Today is the day that Gertie Polpin made her first date with Teddy Heelin. *(takes her hands again)* Now, whisper something nice to me!

GERT Such as?

TEDDY Such as, you like me.

GERT *(whispers)* I like you.

TEDDY And I like you too. I don't suppose you would be inclined to whisper "I love you".

GERT It's a bit early for that, isn't it?

TEDDY But it's possible you will say it?

GERT All things are possible.

TEDDY *(seriously)* When the day comes that you say that, I will be a very happy fellow.

GERT See you're here at half-seven.

TEDDY Is that an order?

GERT It is!

TEDDY Well, I can tell you, Miss Polpin, that it's the most valuable order I've had since I became a commercial traveller. I suppose you intend to reform me?

GERT Well, since you ask, it's only fair to tell you that it's the highest notion in my head. Do you mind?

TEDDY I'm going to enjoy it.

GERT It won't be easy.

TEDDY Come on, give us another kiss, and I'll give you a free pair of garters.

GERT You're terrible.

(They kiss briefly)

You know I think you are a really nice fellow at heart and that what they say about you is not all true.

TEDDY *(seriously)* I'm not like this with anybody else. I want you to know that. I haven't a very high opinion of people generally, nor of myself either. I like you though! You're not grown up yet, but I don't mind that! Give us another kiss . . . *(enter Byrne).*

BYRNE Do you know what I forgot?

(Gert and Teddy are surprised).

GERT We don't know, but why don't you tell us?

BYRNE Raisins. Seedless ones. *(to Teddy)* I like a bun sir, with raisins in it. *(to Gert)* Did you get them in? You hadn't them the last time.

GERT *(produces a packet of raisins)* Here they are. I hope you enjoy the buns.

BYRNE Are they seedless?

GERT As far as I know.

BYRNE How much?

GERT Two shillings.

(Byrne hands over the money and examines the raisins).

BYRNE *(to Teddy)* Aren't they cheap now, considering the long journey they come.

(Exit Byrne).

TEDDY Bit nosey isn't he?

GERT He isn't really. He just likes to know things. He's

regarded as the local encyclopaedia. I'd swear he has a notion of my mother.

TEDDY Ah, go on.

GERT I'd better call her.

TEDDY Yes, better. I've a good few calls to make before the post. I haven't much time. *(Gert goes to exit of shop and calls).*

GERT Mother . . . Mother . . . Crawford's traveller is here.

MAGGIE *(faintly from distance)* Who?

GERT Crawford's traveller.

TEDDY You make me sound like a stranger.

GERT You're anything but.

TEDDY How is your mother, by the way?

GERT Never better. She drives now, you know.

TEDDY Oh! When did she learn?

GERT Katie taught her before she married.

TEDDY Your man told me about Katie's marriage. I must say I was surprised.

GERT The wild ones always settle down quickly once they make up their minds.

TEDDY Is she happy?

GERT She seems to be. He's very wealthy, you know. I wouldn't marry him of course. He asked me once, the first time after Katie turned him down.

TEDDY I wouldn't have taken "no" for an answer.

GERT How are you sure the answer would have been "no" when you never asked?

TEDDY How in the name of blazes could I have asked . . . when I . . .

(Enter Maggie. She is dressed in a smart bright frock. She looks younger. Her hair is neat and orderly and she is well made-up).

MAGGIE *(charmingly)* Hello, Mr Heelin. *(shakes hands with him).*

TEDDY Hello, Mrs Polpin. So Katie got married?

56

MAGGIE She would have invited you but we decided to keep it strictly family so soon after the funeral.

TEDDY Of course.

MAGGIE You look well.

TEDDY I must say, Mrs Polpin, that I've never seen you looking better and that isn't just sales-talk!

MAGGIE Do you hear that, Gert? He's looking for an order already.

TEDDY Seriously, Mrs Polpin, I would appreciate the order right away. I'm a little behind schedule.

MAGGIE Well, it's all made out for you together with your cheque.

TEDDY Good.

MAGGIE Gert, like a good girl will you go back to the kitchen and keep an eye on the dinner.

GERT O.K. See you Teddy.

(Blows him a kiss without Maggie's noticing. Exit Gert. Maggie goes behind counter and returns with cheque while Teddy who has taken receipt book from attache case is writing out a receipt. Maggie hands him order and cheque).

MAGGIE Here you are, Teddy. *(gives him the order)* Teddy is your first name, isn't it?

TEDDY That's what people call me.

MAGGIE It's a wonder some nice girl hasn't hooked you before this.

TEDDY The right one didn't come my way yet.

MAGGIE How long were you in the shop before I came out?

TEDDY Oh, about a quarter of an hour or so. Why?

MAGGIE You spent all that time talking to Gert?

TEDDY Yes, but I . . .

MAGGIE She's young, Teddy.

TEDDY She's a woman, Mrs Polpin. Your receipt.

MAGGIE You can call me Maggie. There's no need for the missus. We've known each other a long time. The size of the order you've just received should show you what we think of you here. I regard you as a friend of the family and that's why I'm asking you to leave Gert alone.

TEDDY You make things very awkward for me.

MAGGIE I think we know each other. At least I know a good deal about you. I know for instance, that you're no cock virgin with innocent dreams of romance.

TEDDY By the Lord, you don't mince words.

MAGGIE I don't believe in mincing words.

TEDDY Good. We can be candid then, but how candid is the question.

MAGGIE Be as open as you like. That's the way I like it.

TEDDY The first part of what you said is true, but you're wrong about the second part. I'll be honest with you and tell you that I could very easily fall in love with Gert. I've asked her if she would like to come out tonight and she's willing, and I'm glad, very glad, because I genuinely like her.

MAGGIE You're a good-looking fellow! No doubt she finds you attractive, I honestly can't blame her.

TEDDY Thank you.

MAGGIE You really are attractive and I can see how easy it would be for any woman to fall for you. She's too young for you. You're too assured and too experienced for my Gert. You say you have honourable intentions. Does this mean that you intend to marry her one day?

TEDDY To tell the truth, I hadn't thought about marriage, but with a girl like Gert, it would have to be marriage – wouldn't it?

MAGGIE You mean that she wouldn't allow you into bed with her unless you married her?

TEDDY I wish you wouldn't put it like that, but I suppose you're right.

MAGGIE Let's be honest. Do you desperately want to go to bed with her?

TEDDY Well, that wouldn't be unnatural if I loved her.

MAGGIE But it boils down to the same thing, doesn't it . . . ?

TEDDY It does not! It's more than sex. You want me to be honest. I will! I've fancied other women and wanted to make love to them, and I often did. As far as sex is concerned, I've never really been satisfied. I don't mean I've been frustrated, but something has been missing.

MAGGIE And you think that the thing that has been missing is a girl like Gert, what people call a nice girl?

TEDDY Well . . . yes.

MAGGIE So that's what you think of the women you slept with, they gave you the lot, and all you can say is there was something missing.

TEDDY I'm sorry, I've never thought about it like that.

MAGGIE Men never do! The more a woman gives, the less men think of her. Why don't you continue as you are? Women here and there to give you what you want and no responsibility.

TEDDY You make it sound different than it really is.

MAGGIE Maybe it's your conscience that's at you! Maybe you're beginning to feel guilty at last!

TEDDY That's not it exactly.

MAGGIE *(loudly and angrily)* Then for the love of God explain yourself. Tell me what it is exactly. I know you're honest and that's a rare commodity in a man.

TEDDY Are you blaming me for past mistakes.

MAGGIE I'm not and you know I'm not!

TEDDY I don't usually let women talk to me this way, but you're different, Maggie.

MAGGIE It seems to me that for all your women you're not very happy.

TEDDY Meet a woman, make love to her, and gone the next day – what does it all add up to? I used to promise myself that each time would be the last time. But I was tempted. I used to say maybe this time it's the right one.

MAGGIE Gert?

TEDDY Maybe not. She's a beauty, but maybe I need someone more . . . mature.

MAGGIE Someone with experience, who knows what you want from a woman.

TEDDY Yes . . . It's a bit of a game sometimes.

MAGGIE Romance is for young ones, Teddy. I had my share of it and then my husband gave me a dog's life. For ten years he didn't sleep with me. In the end I didn't want him, but it was a strange and terrible way for a healthy woman to live. I wouldn't tell you this but I feel we understand each other.

TEDDY Ten years . . . that's a long time.

MAGGIE Sometimes it doesn't matter.

TEDDY And other times? . . . I hate to think of anyone being unhappy. There's no reason for it now, you're free.

MAGGIE No one knows that better than me.

TEDDY You can have the things you want now. Do what you like. Who's to stop you?

MAGGIE No one.

TEDDY God knows I'm not giving you advice – I been in too many scrapes myself and there were times things happened I was sorry for afterwards.

MAGGIE Sure, that's what life is. That's the way men are. I know.

TEDDY Of course you know, you've great understanding. You know how a man needs a woman – and a woman needs a man. It's something we both understand.

MAGGIE Yes.

TEDDY There aren't many women with your honesty. You won't be hurt if I say this –

MAGGIE I'm not easily hurt any more.

TEDDY Sometimes a man and a woman, they have the same need – the same longing. It can happen quickly, they don't need any romantic games. They know.

MAGGIE No one can blame people for what they are.

TEDDY Sometimes a man can see a woman and want her more than anyone ever before. He wonders if she thinks the same?

MAGGIE She might – if she thought the same about him.

TEDDY How would he know?

MAGGIE That would be for him to find out.

TEDDY You're a remarkable woman. I'd like to really understand you.

MAGGIE You will. Time to close for dinner.

TEDDY All the times I've come in here and talked to you and I never really knew you until now. That sounds like sales talk but I mean it – I don't think I've felt this way with any woman before.

MAGGIE Maybe you've never met a woman like me before.

TEDDY I don't know what it is about you – but for once I'm not sure of myself.

MAGGIE I want you to be yourself.

(He kisses her, she does not resist).

TEDDY When can I see you . . . alone I mean?

MAGGIE When do you want to see me?

TEDDY The sooner the better. Tonight!

MAGGIE Tonight, then.

TEDDY Tonight.

MAGGIE What time?

TEDDY Whatever time you say.

MAGGIE Nine o'clock. I'll have everything done by then.

TEDDY It's such a long way off!

MAGGIE It will be worth waiting for. Go now.

TEDDY Oh God!

MAGGIE What is it?

TEDDY What about Gert?

MAGGIE Let me worry about Gert. She's only a child. Her fancies don't last.

TEDDY Perhaps I should tell her that I'm breaking our date?

MAGGIE No! Don't worry about it! I'll take care of everything. You'd better finish off your calls. I don't want you to be late.

TEDDY I won't be late. Till tonight then.

MAGGIE Till tonight.

TEDDY Right. Till tonight.

(Exit Teddy).

(Maggie takes lipstick tube from her pocket and applies it to her lips).

MAGGIE *(calls)* Gert! *(pause, louder)* Gert!

GERT *(off)* In a minute.

MAGGIE *(calls to Gert again)* Gert!

GERT *(off)* Coming!

MAGGIE Never mind . . . It was just something I was looking for . . . I found it.

CURTAIN
for end of Scene I, Act II

ACT TWO

Scene Two

The shop is empty. Byrne passes the door, pauses, then enters. He knocks on the counter, changes his mind and exits, as he does Maurice enters from house and sees him go. Maurice carries a bucket. He crosses to the meal sack S.L., then he bends down behind the counter for the meal scoop. Byrne returns and again knocks on the S.R. counter – unaware of Maurice.

MAURICE *(rising)* Yes?

BYRNE *(surprised)* Good evening.

MAURICE Good evening.

BYRNE I was passing.

MAURICE So I saw.

BYRNE I came in.

MAURICE Can I get you something?

BYRNE Herself.

MAURICE My mother?

BYRNE Who else.

MAURICE I'll call her. *(to D.R. door)* Mother, Mr Byrne's here to see you.

MAGGIE In a minute.

MAURICE She'll be with you in a minute. *(pause)* I'm only getting a few scoops of meal for a weak ewe. We're near closing.

BYRNE The shop's doing well this past while.

MAURICE Could be better.

BYRNE How about your end – the farm?

MAURICE Could be worse.

BYRNE That's something in these hard times.

MAURICE Hard times is right, according to my mother anyway.

BYRNE She'll know best.

MAURICE None better – according to herself.

BYRNE Your mother is like strong medicine – hard to take sometimes but 'twill do you good in the long run.

MAURICE How long is the long run.

BYRNE You mean the young Madden one I suppose? A nice little girl. I do see the two of you some evenings heading for Kelvey's Wood.

MAURICE Sometimes you see to much, Mr Byrne.

BYRNE Could be. But I've more time on me hands now with the style of tombstones getting smaller. I often sit on the graveyard wall remembering past generations, contemplating the present one and having a shot at spotting where the future generation will come from.

MAURICE It's easy for you to make jokes but if you were in my shoes you'd wonder if there was going to be any future generation at all.

BYRNE If I was in your shoes, Maurice, I'd learn how to lace them myself and not have my mother always tying them for me.

MAURICE You don't know my mother.

BYRNE I wasn't talking about your mother, I was talking about you.

(Maggie enters).

MAGGIE Maurice, did you mark that meal on a slip of paper and put it in the till?

MAURICE I did. Would you like it signed by the Minister of Agriculture?

MAGGIE If it meant keeping my books straight for the tax man I would. Off with you now and if I'm in bed before you get back I'll leave the key under the stone. *(Exit Maurice).*

MAGGIE Well, Byrne?

BYRNE Good evening, Maggie.

64

MAGGIE Oh, good evening to you too. Was it you I saw walking up and down past the door earlier.

BYRNE Could be.

MAGGIE What's the matter with you now?

BYRNE I won't put a tooth in it. I came to put my cards on the table.

MAGGIE You'll have to postpone the game, Byrne, because I'm otherwise engaged as of now.

BYRNE I won't keep you two minutes.

MAGGIE *(thoughtfully)* Two minutes. O.K. Fire away! But be brief and busy about it or I'll show you the door!

BYRNE Now that I have my chance I don't know where to begin.

MAGGIE For a beginning, I may tell you that you're doing a lot of arseing around here lately.

BYRNE I don't deny I'm around here more than I should.

MAGGIE I've noticed you for the past few weeks like a gander that would badly want to gattle a goose.

BYRNE I suppose that's one way of putting it.

MAGGIE Only the other night I was saying to myself. Byrne is looking a bit hot and bothered, and says I, Byrne is behaving more like a jackdaw than a monumental sculptor.

BYRNE You've had your say. It's my turn now. I have four thousand pounds in the bank.

MAGGIE I'm not surprised, the prices you charge for headstones.

BYRNE I'm a man of sober habits, although I take a drink if the occasion calls for it, and I have no objection to a woman taking a drink either. I'm a steady worker and there is wide demand for my work. I'm a good Catholic and I does the Nine Fridays regular. I never missed Mass in my life and there's no year I don't earn more than would keep a family in comfort. I am told by folk that should know, that I am the best

E

monumental sculptor around these parts.

MAGGIE You're a monumental eejit, if you ask me.

BYRNE Well! Will you or won't you?

MAGGIE Will I or won't I what?

BYRNE Marry me.

MAGGIE Marry you?

BYRNE Yes.

MAGGIE Were you ever at the zoo, Byrne?

BYRNE I was, the year of the Eucharistic Congress when I was in Dublin. That was 1932. I was a young man then. But what has the zoo got to do with it?

MAGGIE Well, Byrne, if you were at the zoo, you know what a baboon is?

BYRNE *(innocently)* I daresay I do.

MAGGIE Good for you, because, Byrne, I would sooner be buckled to a baboon than buckled to you.

BYRNE You're an insulting woman!
(He goes towards exit. As he does, Teddy Heelin enters).

BYRNE A baboon would suit you all right. The bother is, Maggie, that no self-respecting mother of a monkey would consent to a son of hers marrying you.

MAGGIE I'll hand it to you, Byrne. You gave me my answer.

BYRNE Die, Maggie, and I'll give you a Celtic Cross for nothing. *(to Teddy)* Good night to you, sir.
(Exit Byrne).

TEDDY *(laughs)* What was all that about?

MAGGIE Believe it or not, Teddy Heelin, I've had a proposal of marriage.

TEDDY And did you say yes?

MAGGIE I've had my fair quota of marriage, thank you. What's the time?

TEDDY Time? It's only just nine. Where's Gert?

MAGGIE She's gone to see Katie.

TEDDY Good. Was she disappointed when I didn't show up?

MAGGIE Very. Wait until I close this door. Anyone could walk in.

TEDDY We certainly don't want that.

MAGGIE I like a man who is punctual. I wasn't sure whether you would change your mind or not, so I'm not fully ready for you.

TEDDY One look at you and I know you're ready for me. Come here!

(She goes to him).

I've thought about you all day. I made several mistakes when I was totting my returns in the hotel and that's something I never do. As well as that I forgot two calls.

MAGGIE Are you just saying that!

TEDDY I missed you! Let me show you how much! *(He puts his arms around her and kisses her. She responds and they draw apart to survey each other).*

MAGGIE You're so uncomplicated. *(They kiss again).*

TEDDY Let's not stay here much longer.

MAGGIE Whatever you say.

TEDDY Let's go upstairs.

MAGGIE You're in a terrible hurry.

TEDDY Yes, I am!

MAGGIE Do you want to go upstairs now?

TEDDY What do you think?

(He takes her in his arms and kisses her, fondling her as he does so. She doesn't resist. She does not respond. Enter Gert silently. Teddy is kissing Maggie passionately).

TEDDY *(to Maggie)* I've never known a woman like you! It's more than love and it's more than lust. You have become an obsession with me. I don't know how to put it. You overwhelm me. My head is light when I hold you! Yet I never dreamed it could be possible with you. How could I have been so blind!

GERT *(looking away)* Mother!

(Teddy looks around foolishly and sees Gert. He breaks with Maggie).

GERT Was this the reason you sent me with the messages to Katie. Was it?

(Maggie does not reply).

GERT Was he the reason you sent me to Katie's? *(to Teddy)* You know what she did? She sent me off to Katie's twenty minutes ago. She told me to hurry back again. She told me she wanted me for something else. I know you played about, Teddy Heelin, but I had no idea you would stoop to do a dreadful thing like this!

TEDDY Believe me, Gert, I'm, I . . .

GERT Two-faced isn't the word for you, and as for you, Mother. You let him kiss you! How could you do such a thing!

MAGGIE Aren't you forgetting something?

GERT What do you mean!

MAGGIE I'm single now, the same as you.

GERT I hate you!

MAGGIE You shouldn't! Any girl with an ounce of sense would thank me. If you had your own way you'd make a complete wreck of your life.

GERT And is it how you think it's not wrecked now?

MAGGIE God help you, child, a small scratch is all you got. 'Twill be healed in a week at your age.

GERT You're welcome to him, you're a rotten pair! The two of you.

(Exit Gert).

TEDDY You shouldn't have done that.

MAGGIE Do you think I liked doing it.

TEDDY Christ, it was a cruel thing to do.

MAGGIE She'll get over it, she won't travel the same road I did. You won't get the chance to treat her like the dirt under your feet. She'll think twice before she falls for your kind again. That's what happened to me. The man I married lived exactly the way you are living now. When we married everyone said he'd change, but he didn't change. If anything he was worse.

TEDDY You made a fool of me.

MAGGIE You did it to yourself. You take it for granted that every woman is dying to fall into your arms. When I saw the way things were going I just let it happen.

TEDDY You shamed me. No matter what I am or what I was, no one has the right to do that to another human being.

MAGGIE Don't give me that stuff about human beings, because that's the biggest lie of all. If a man or woman hasn't self respect they have nothing. You should know that, because you are nothing, you have nothing, and God pity you, you never will.

CURTAIN
for end of Act II

Act Three

SCENE ONE
The Shop—almost a year later

SCENE TWO
That night

ACT THREE

Scene One

Action as before.
The time is the evening of a day almost a year later.
Maggie is behind the counter. Katie with a pram is on the outside. Maggie is totting a list of messages.

MAGGIE The whole lot amounts to six pounds one and sevenpence.

KATIE I'll pay you now. Himself will call for them to-night. *(Katie accepts and checks list. Indignant)* Are you going to charge me full price for everything?

MAGGIE Why not? Don't you want me to make a profit? We can't all be married to millionaires you know.

KATIE You'll throw off the one and sevenpence anyway!

MAGGIE I'll throw off nothing. Fork out six pounds one and sevenpence like a good girl. I'm running a shop, not a relieving office. *(Katie locates money in handbag and hands it to Maggie)*.

KATIE What will you do with all the money you have?

MAGGIE I have no money!

KATIE Ah, stop!

MAGGIE *(simply)* I have no money but I have my health. How would I have money with supermarkets sprouting up everywhere like daisies? I have enough for myself though. I can tell you that. You see I never got anything from anybody and I don't see who's going to give to me now, unless maybe yourself.

KATIE There's no one your match!

MAGGIE If I was looking at that baby from here till Doomsday I couldn't make out who he takes after.

KATIE There's no telling at that age. He's like his father sometimes and sometimes like his mother.

MAGGIE I happen to know the mother and there's no likeness. Maybe he's like his father. I wouldn't know about that of course.

KATIE God Almighty, you're a terrible woman!

MAGGIE Katie, a woman would want the character of Saint Brigid in this country to get away with a seven months' birth.

KATIE Meaning what?

MAGGIE Meaning you're no Saint Brigid. What are you feeding the child?

KATIE The pasteurised of course.

MAGGIE There's no nature in children since they stopped the breast feeding. Women these days don't seem to know what tits are for. In my day every child was fed from the breast.

KATIE Well, if you were fed from the breast, mother mine, it didn't give you much nature.

MAGGIE That tongue of yours will get you into trouble one of these days. 'Tis a wonder your husband doesn't take a stick to you.

KATIE If he did I'd cripple him with a poker.

MAGGIE I don't doubt you!

KATIE Did you hear anything from Gert since she left?

MAGGIE Not a word.

KATIE Maurice had a letter from her.

MAGGIE If he had he never said it to me.

KATIE She told him in the letter to tell you nothing.

MAGGIE What's she at over there?

KATIE She's doing nursing. She's in a flat with Mick.

MAGGIE Nursing . . . See now, wasn't I for her good?

KATIE What happened the night before she ran away?

MAGGIE That's none of your business, Madam. But since you're so curious, it was the beginning of her education. I gave her the matriculation, you might say.

'Twas the best bit of schooling she's ever likely to get.

KATIE Maybe 'twas a bit too severe. She left in a terrible hurry.

MAGGIE Nothing is too severe for what she'll meet in this world. Nothing.

KATIE Have you any notion of letting Maurice get married?

MAGGIE To the Madden one is it?

KATIE Who else?

MAGGIE The day she lobs up fifteen hundred pounds on that counter I'll be the first woman to dance at her wedding.

KATIE Mary Madden is a nice girl and Maurice has his heart set on her.

MAGGIE You should pass that information on to the bank manager and see how much you'll get for it.

KATIE I'm telling you in time. Maurice won't wait much longer. He's determined and he's been pushed as far as he'll go.

(Enter Byrne).

MAGGIE Byrne! I thought we'd never again see you.

BYRNE I'm like my monuments, Maggie! Takes more than a gale of wind to flatten one of them. Katie, how are you? *(he shakes hands with her).*

KATIE I'm fine, Mr Byrne, thank you. How's yourself?

BYRNE Carrying the day the best I can, Katie! Maggie, throw us out a half quarter of tobacco. *(puts money on the counter. Looking into pram)* Is this the gorsoon? He's like you, Katie. God bless the child!

KATIE Thank you, Mr Byrne.

(Byrne continues to peer at the child).

KATIE *(to Maggie)* Have you any notion of getting in a few girls to help you?

MAGGIE My experience of girls is that they only come in the way.

KATIE Very funny.

MAGGIE Isn't it though, when you think about it.

KATIE You'll never manage all the work alone.

MAGGIE Meaning of course that I should let the Madden one in.

KATIE She's a topping worker, Mother, and a marvellous milker.

MAGGIE Well, if she is she won't milk my cows. In the honour of God, Byrne, give the child a pound or two. Do you see him with his lousy half crown giving it to the child.

BYRNE Silver is the done thing.

MAGGIE If that's your case, show me up a fiver and I'll change it into silver for you.

BYRNE You're very free with other people's money. I bet you weren't so liberal with the child yourself.

KATIE Good for you, Byrne!
(Enter Old Man and Woman who were seen at the churchyard earlier).

OLD WOMAN God bless all. *(they acknowledge her salute)* Give us a pound of sugar please, Missus.

MAGGIE Shag off outa here and get your sugar where you get your tea. There's no profit on sugar. Here's your tobacco, Byrne.

BYRNE *(accepting it)* That's no way to talk to those old people. You should be ashamed of yourself.

MAGGIE The same applies to you if you don't like the situation here.

BYRNE God bless you, but you have a heart of limestone.

MAGGIE Wouldn't I want it, to be dealing with the likes of you. Where were you, Byrne, and where was everyone else when I had my back to the wall?
(Old Man and Old Woman are examining the baby).

OLD WOMAN Is it a boy or a girl?

KATIE 'Tis a boy.

OLD MAN He's a healthy little rascal 'faith! What do you call him?

76

KATIE He's called Michael after his Uncle Mick.

OLD MAN How's Mick doing now?

KATIE Very well, thank you.

OLD WOMAN And Gert? What way is Gert?

KATIE She's doing nursing.

OLD MAN A nurse is handy. No family should be without a nurse.

OLD WOMAN *(to Katie)* And yourself, missus, how're you keeping?

KATIE Fine, thank you.

OLD WOMAN Is he showing any sign of a tooth?

MAGGIE Go on away now and don't be addling us. If you want any more information buy the papers.

OLD MAN *(to Old Woman)* Come on away! *(the Old Woman moves towards the door. The Old Man takes a final look into the pram)* Well, there's one consolation anyway. He don't look one bit like his grandmother.
(Exit Old Man and Old Woman).

KATIE You had that coming.

MAGGIE Those two came for information. 'Tis their passport into the public house. They must be in a right stew around the countryside trying to figure out what's going here.

KATIE How would outside people know when a daughter of the house hasn't a clue.

MAGGIE Byrne, do you want any more messages?

BYRNE *(raises his hand)* Don't worry, I'm leaving. So long, Katie!

KATIE Goodbye, Mr Byrne.

BYRNE By the way, Maggie, that offer I made you still stands.

MAGGIE Like the monuments you're always boasting about, Byrne. 'Twill be standing for ever.
(Exit Byrne).

KATIE What does he mean by that?

MAGGIE He wants to marry me.

77

KATIE Ah, go on!

MAGGIE He proposed.

KATIE If he has any sense he'll stay single.

MAGGIE Maybe 'tis your own story you're telling.

KATIE What difference does it make to me now – I'm tied and there's damn all I can do about it. Still, it could be worse. I have my own car and I handle the money. I have independence and that's more than most wives have.

MAGGIE And you have that eejit of a servant boy drooling after you like a stud greyhound. Watch yourself of that fellow! He wouldn't be long cooling your radiator.

KATIE I can't help it if I excite his interest.

MAGGIE Cut that out now, do you hear! I'm still capable of coming outside the counter and putting you in your place.

KATIE You wouldn't dare touch me now, my mother.

MAGGIE I'll touch you if I see the need for it. Be certain of that.

KATIE To change the subject. What really brought me here this evening was to talk to you about Maurice.

MAGGIE Will you ever learn to mind your own business.

KATIE He asked me and I made him a promise I'd talk to you.

MAGGIE Go on!

KATIE Johnny would secure him for the money if you hand over the place.

MAGGIE What kind of an ape do you take me for? I haven't the place a year yet and you want me to sign it over already.

KATIE It's not fair to Maurice, Mother. How could he pay back the money he borrowed if he wasn't boss?

MAGGIE It would be less fair to me, Katie. As far as I can see everyone is anxious to forget about that.

KATIE Here he is now.

MAGGIE Here is he who now?

78

KATIE Maurice.

MAGGIE Ah, so that's it! You came in to pave the way, to soften me out! You'll soften an anvil with soap-suds quicker than you'll soften me.

(Enter Maurice. Maggie produces a cigarette and lights it).

KATIE Give us a fag.

MAGGIE Buy your own. You have more than I have.

MAURICE Well?

KATIE *(hopelessly)* I've done my best, Maurice.

MAURICE Mother, I want to get married.

MAGGIE I know, son. Katie told me.

MAURICE A year ago you told me to wait, that God was good. Well, Mother, God has turned out to be no good but maybe that's because you're not giving Him much of a chance.

MAGGIE I can't understand why you have this awful rush on you to get married. I look after you well, don't I? I wouldn't mind you marrying if you had no one to look after you. If I was dead you'd need a woman to help you run the place. There would be some sense to that but there's no sense at all to this carry-on.

MAURICE Now, Mother, you asked me to wait and I've waited a whole year, and I would much prefer Mary Madden to look after me than you, meaning no disrespect. I'm not getting younger you know.

MAGGIE Wait another year and I'll see what way the land lies then. You're too young for the present.

MAURICE That's what you told me last year and by the looks of things that's what you'll be telling me every year till I'm an old man.

MAGGIE I know I asked you to wait, Maurice, and now I'm asking you to wait again for a while anyway. Try to have patience.

MAURICE My patience is at an end.

MAGGIE I'm for your own good. Must I always be telling you that? For your good I am!

KATIE Don't listen to her, Maurice! It must be now or never!

MAGGIE If I hear another word out of you out you go! A while ago you said a person was better off single. If you take my advice, Maurice, and I know you will, you'll be in no hurry to give up your freedom. I know what I'm talking about! 'Tis only now I know what freedom means.

MAURICE But, Mother, I can't wait any longer. Unless you grant me permission I'll join Mick and Gert in England. It's no bother to get married there.

MAGGIE Oh, no bother at all, and less bother to live in one dirty room for the rest of your life. What sort of job do you think you'll get . . . You have no training for anything but the pick and shovel. Here you're the same as the best in the land and there's something thought of you.

MAURICE Johnny Conlon will put up the security for the money you want. He'll do it the minute you agree.

MAGGIE And then Dan Madden's snotty-nosed daughter takes over here. Nothing doing! 'Tisn't the Colleen Bawn you're playing with.

MAURICE In that case, it's England for me.

MAGGIE Listen to me now, Maurice, like a good boy. You have a good home here. You're not short of money. Haven't I always given you enough? Have I or haven't I? Have I ever been mean with you as long as you know me!

MAURICE All I know is that I'm in love with Mary Madden and I want to marry her.

MAGGIE And will you be in love with her when she's trying to rear three or four children in a poke of a flat! When she starts to get fat and irritable and has no time to dress up or do her hair? When her teeth start getting bad, when her belly is swollen and her nose starts to run?

MAURICE Don't say that!

MAGGIE Every goddam one of her mother's seed and breed had snotty noses and big backsides like bullocks before they were thirty.

MAURICE You're impossible.

MAGGIE When you have four or five kids and start to run short of money, you'll remember me and your fine car and your wardrobe of clothes and you'll curse Mary Madden for the conniving little vixen she is. What makes you think she sees anything in you. If you were a labouring man she wouldn't pass you the time of day.

MAURICE I don't have to listen to this. Who's going to look after the land and milk the cows? You'll get no one to work as I did.

MAGGIE I'll sell the cows and I'll let the land. You'll be the one to lose, not me.

MAURICE I've given my whole life to that farm and this is what I get in the end.

MAGGIE 'Tis your own choice, not mine. I don't want you to leave but you'll have to choose between me and Mary Madden.

KATIE Mother, he means what he's saying.

MAGGIE So do I!

KATIE Don't give in, Maurice.

MAURICE I'm going out now to tidy up the yard and that's the last stroke of work you'll ever get out of me.

MAGGIE Go on. You don't appreciate what I'm trying to do for you!

MAURICE *(exiting)* The quicker I go now, the better. I'm only wasting time.
(Exit Maurice).

KATIE You're hard.

MAGGIE 'Tis the hardness of concern. Always remember that about me.

KATIE To be fair to you I know now that there's an

F

element of truth in what you said to him.

MAGGIE Aha! My first convert!

KATIE Oh no, I'm not! Things can be like you say, but they needn't be if you let him stay here.

MAGGIE But I want him to stay here!

KATIE But without Mary Madden.

MAGGIE You know the conditions.

KATIE It's a waste of time arguing with you!

MAGGIE I'm glad to see you're getting a bit of sense. *(Katie turns pram towards exit).*

KATIE Mick is gone. Gert is gone and now Maurice is going and he won't come back.

MAGGIE Have a good look and see if you can notice any tears on my face.

KATIE But you'll be all alone here, completely alone.

MAGGIE Don't be too sure. What's to stop me from marrying Byrne? He has four thousand pounds in the bank.

KATIE Don't be ridiculous.

MAGGIE What's ridiculous about it? Byrne is no chicken. He won't live for ever, and if Byrne goes, there's plenty left for another one after him.

KATIE You're not serious.

MAGGIE Look, child of grace, I'm busy. I have to scrub out the shop so if you have any more to say, say it quick and go home and get your husband's supper.

KATIE I have one last thing to say to you, Mother.

MAGGIE Say it!

KATIE If you don't change your mind about Maurice I'll never come here again.

MAGGIE Suit yourself.

KATIE You'll have no one.

MAGGIE Won't I be lucky if 'tis true for you but you'll never give it to say to the neighbours. You're too high up in the world, girl, to have them gossiping about you.

KATIE About me? About you, you mean!

MAGGIE Why would they gossip about me? I placed you well and gave you a good fortune. No, 'tis you they'll talk about. They'll say, isn't she the thankless hussy that don't go to see her poor mother. Look at the bitch, they'll say, in her sports car and the mother still working like a slave.

KATIE You still have time to change your mind.

MAGGIE Clear out of my sight and let me at my work.

KATIE Have you any feeling at all for me?

MAGGIE How can you ask that, when you know I saved you from disgrace.

KATIE But have you any feeling of love for me?

MAGGIE I have! I have it for all of you. That's why I never let any of you have your own way. If I hadn't love I wouldn't care.

KATIE But you are ruining Maurice's life, Mother, yet you won't see it that way. I'm going, but know this for certain, you'll never see me in this house again.

MAGGIE Good luck to you, girl.

(Katie wheels pram towards exit).

KATIE Have you any last thing to say to me before I go?

MAGGIE I have!

(Katie waits for it).

Since you won't be coming yourself don't forget to send somebody else up for your messages.

(Exit Katie).

fade out
CURTAIN
for end of Scene I, Act III

ACT THREE

Scene Two

Action takes place as before.
The time is that night.
Maggie is seated on a high stool with a ledger in front of her.
She is in the act of sending out bills. Suddenly she rises and
goes to the phone. Twists handle and lifts the receiver.

MAGGIE Hallo . . . Hallo . . . *(louder)* Hallo . . . I thought
you were gone to bed. Will you get me the Whacker
Flynn's . . . please. I'll hold on. Hallo! Hallo Whacker,
I'm fine thank you, but I'd be a lot finer, Whacker, if
you paid your bill. *(she listens)* Last month you said
you'd send it tomorrow and the month before that, you
said you'd send it tomorrow. It's there now with over a
year and as far as I can see you have no intention what-
soever of paying it. *(listens)* No need, I'll spare you the
price of a stamp. I'll be over in a quarter of an hour for
it, so you'd better have it for me. *(listens)*.
*(Enter a girl in her early twenties. She wears a coat which
gives her a look of simplicity. Maggie notices her but says
nothing).*
(to phone) I've heard all that before, Whacker, and if
your wife is pregnant again, 'tisn't me that's to blame
for it.
*(The girl who is looking around the shop curiously is Mary
Madden).*
(listens) Ah, sure we all know that you can't get blood
out of a turnip, but it would be an easy matter for me
to drive a cow out of your stall. *(listens while she takes
stock of Mary Madden)* All right, I'll give you an hour

85

but if you aren't here by then I'll be over and I'll note you. *(listens)* And good luck to you too boy.

(Maggie puts down receiver).

MARY Good evening, Mrs Polpin.

MAGGIE Good evening.

MARY *(shyly)* I suppose you don't know me.

MAGGIE How do you know I don't?

MARY *(uncertainly)* Well, we've never met before.

MAGGIE That's true.

MARY I was going to sympathize with you in the grave-yard when your husband died, but I didn't want to be forward.

MAGGIE I see.

(Maggie indicates stool).

Sit down here where I can have a look at you.

(Mary goes and sits on stool, uncomfortably).

That's better!

MARY I suppose I'd better introduce myself.

MAGGIE No. There's no need for that.

MARY Oh!

MAGGIE To tell you the God's honest truth, I was kind of expecting you.

MARY Were you? I suppose I should have called before this but I'm terribly shy. *(gushes on)* It was in my head to call several times but when I was about to start out, something always stopped me. I don't know what it was. I just couldn't bring myself to do it. But I'm really astonished that you should know me, especially since you never laid eyes on me before.

MAGGIE I had a good look at you when you came in the door and I said to myself, who's this one now, and before I had the phone out of my hand I knew you and I knew your business. This is Mary Madden, I said to myself, and by all the laws her mother isn't far behind her.

MARY She's outside talking to Maurice, they made me

come here. I didn't want to but they made me. Maybe I shouldn't have come at all, but it had to be done, I suppose.

MAGGIE Yerra, don't upset yourself, girl. 'Tis a thing of nothing. Says I to myself, she came as soon as she could. She's three or four months gone, now, I said, and that's the only card the poor girl has in her hand. How many is it? Three or four or maybe it's only two? *(Mary doesn't answer)* Ah, come on now Mary, you can surely tell me, but remember, whatever you tell me, you won't fool me.

MARY *(astonished and hurt)* How did you know?

MAGGIE Don't give me any credit. Any one would know! 'Tis what I would call the inevitable.

MARY *(incredulous)* The inevitable?

MAGGIE Exactly. You see it's inevitable because it always happens after everything else fails. You don't show. I'll say that for you, but you can't keep it in for ever, can you?

MARY No, I can't.

MAGGIE God help us, yes child. You can't. 'Tis no fun to be carrying a child without a licence.

MARY You're not angry?

MAGGIE Why would I be angry? What has it got to do with me? I have no right to be angry with you.

MARY Oh, so that's the way is it?

MAGGIE That's the way it is exactly. Whenever I see a poorly-off slip of a girl like yourself now, knocking around with a well-off young lad, I do be on the look-out for it, so to speak.

MARY I can see that I'll get no sympathy from you.

MAGGIE Well, if sympathy was all you wanted I'd give you an assload of it, but I would say you're after more than sympathy.

MARY You're too clever for me.

MAGGIE Maybe, that's because you put all your eggs in

one basket and I didn't. Wouldn't I be in a nice way now if I had signed over to Maurice before this! I'd be a walking tragedy girl, dependent on the likes of you for my breakfast, supper and tea, and old before my time trying to judge your fads and humours, thankful for every hand-out and afraid of my sacred life for fear I might do something or say something to offend your ladyship.

MARY That's not true at all.

MAGGIE God blast you! Use your imagination! Don't you see the way old women are treated by their daughters-in-law the minute they hand over?

MARY You don't have to go on.

MAGGIE (dropping all subtlety) Wouldn't it be a marvellous victory for you and for your mother if I was willing to hand over. Think of it! This fine house and farm, and maybe money too, because they all say I have it, and they can't all be wrong. You'd be a lady of the manor and could have the mother to advise you, and maybe your young sisters to help you in the shop. Did you ever dream that way? Did you? Was that the way you thought it would be?

MARY All I ever wanted was to marry Maurice and I swear that before God.

MAGGIE It's costing you nothing to swear and God is often deaf.

MARY I wanted Maurice. I want him more than ever now and what's his by right.

MAGGIE Well, now you can have what you want, because I daresay the poor fool will want to do the right thing by you. You tried hard all along until you thought of the final number. You must have given it a lot of thought but then you figured that I was no sop on the road and you knew that you'd have to go for a goal if you were to have any kind of chance.

MARY I'm going out and I'll send my mother in for you.

I'm no match for you. **Wha**t people say about you is true!

MAGGIE A snail's tail is small, but I wouldn't give it, small as it is, for what people think of me.

MARY Goodbye.

MAGGIE No, you don't. You'll stay where you are. When I'm finished with you I'll let you know.

MARY Oh, but I'm finished with you.

MAGGIE You'll stay where you are! Did you weigh up the odds well before you decided to surrender yourself? What were the odds? This house, this farm and all that go with them for a minute of madness in the back of a motor car? The odds were high and by God they were worth taking a chance for. But I know your type well, you brazen bitch, and I'd wipe the floor with you before I'd give you the washing of a plate here.

MARY *(coldly)* You won't wipe the floor with me. I can tell you that right now. I'm not one of your children, your softies that can be bullied or frightened.

MAGGIE You're not as soft as you look! I know that well, but I knew it all along the way you held on to him. You have gumption enough to get what you want, but by the Lord God, you won't get it off me! And don't go too far with me, because as soon as I'd look at you, I'd give you a pound weight between the eyes and there's no one would blame me, because I'm entitled to respect under my own roof.

MARY *(changing her tactics)* I'm sorry. You're right. I shouldn't talk back to you in your own house.

MAGGIE Amn't I the lucky woman though, that it is my own house! Amn't I? What chance would I have against you if it was your house? You'd give me short shrift if I had signed over to Maurice.

MARY Maybe we started off on the wrong foot!

MAGGIE It isn't how we started. All that matters is the way we finish.

MARY I couldn't agree more.

MAGGIE I'm happy to hear you say that, because I understand you perfectly and I think you understand me.

MARY I'm trying to!

MAGGIE Well, if you are, I'll give you all the help you need and tell you right now that the interview is over.

MARY My mother will want to say something to you. She's coming in now.

MAGGIE You had a right to bring your grandmother too, for all the good it will do you.

MARY Come in, Mother.

(Enter Mrs Madden and Maurice. She is an able, dumpy-looking woman of fifty in coat and hat, carrying handbag).

MRS MADDEN Well, Maggie Polpin, have you decided what you're going to do about my daughter?

MAGGIE She's your daughter, mam!

MARY You're only wasting your time, Mother, if you expect this woman to do anything decent!

MRS MADDEN I'll be the best judge of that. Answer my question, Maggie Polpin! What do you intend to do about my daughter?

MAGGIE As I said before, my good woman, she's your daughter.

MRS MADDEN But your son is to be the father of her child!

MAGGIE Well, then it's his look-out, not mine.

MRS MADDEN I'm not leaving here till there's a settlement. We have a right to that!

MAGGIE You have a right to nothing.

(Mrs Madden folds her arms and assumes a belligerent stance).

MRS MADDEN Come down off your high horse, or you'll be the sorry woman. I'm telling you now, and I'm giving you advance notice that you're up against the wrong crowd in the Maddens. The grass will grow on the road to your shop from the boycotting we'll give you.

MAGGIE You boycott me or let a member of your family stand outside my door and I'll fix them quick.

MRS MADDEN And how, pray, would you do that? *(Exit Maggie. Returns with double-barrelled gun)*.

MAGGIE Do you see this? I know how to use it. Let one of your breed so much as stand within an asses' roar of my shop and you'll be picking buckshot out of their arses for the next ten years.

MAURICE Mrs Madden, there's no point in going any farther with her. I know her! I should have known better than to expect you to have any success with her.

MAGGIE Poor Maurice.

MAURICE I'll be in England in a week and I'll be married and I'll never be back here again! *(he goes to Mary's side)*.

MRS MADDEN I'm not yielding an inch till she does the right thing by my daughter that I reared well. I didn't rear her for England.

MAGGIE Maurice, if you have any sense you'll have no more to do with this gang. Break with them now, boy, because 'tis the last chance you'll ever have!

MAURICE How can you say such a thing! What would happen to Mary? What would happen to the child? My child!

MAGGIE Let Mrs Madden here figure that one out. I'm sure it would be no bother to her.

MAURICE Have you any bit of consideration at all. *(near to tears)* Have you any feelings! You are driving me out of my father's house, out of the home where I was born and reared. *(to all)* I hate going! I hate it! I hate it! I hate it! I'm a grown man and yet I have nothing, no money, no home, no land. *(slowly repeats through clenched teeth)* Who can I thank for it all? My own mother!

MARY No, Maurice. No! *(comfortingly)* We'll be all right.

MAGGIE *(coldly)* There is no one forcing you to go, Maurice.

MAURICE *(vehemently)* No! No one only you that has an answer for everything. *(to Mary)* I'll get the car around and drive you home. I won't be a minute.
(Exit Maurice).

MARY Now I see what you're really like I'll give him the happiness you never gave him, I'll see that he's happy from now on.

MAGGIE That should have been your plan without coming here tonight. It's no use saying it to me! It's you he wants, or rather it's you he thinks he wants. *(to Mrs Madden)* You had a hand in this too, and I'm not going to acquit you so easily. Maurice was always happy here till your daughter came along. We'll see now how happy he'll be in the years to come! It's his choice and your choice, but not mine. I want him here but you've come around him nicely between the pair of you.

MRS MADDEN I wouldn't waste my breath on you!

MAGGIE Yerra shag off outa that! I'm sick of you! The cheek of you to come barging like a circus elephant into my house!

MARY There's a long road ahead of us and it's ahead of you too, but if he ever gives in, in the years ahead and wants to come and see you, I'll stop him, and when you're on your death bed, I'll stop him and I'll get him to stop the others too! I can do it!

MAGGIE I know well what you can do, but devil the use any one of them will be to me when I'm on my death bed.

MRS MADDEN Come on, Mary! The car is outside. It was a journey for nothing!

MARY Maybe so! But at least Maurice lost his temper there for a minute, and I've never seen him do that before. He turned into a man there of a sudden!

MAGGIE If he did, it's me he can thank for it, not you two!

MARY You really believe that, don't you?

MAGGIE I do!

MRS MADDEN *(to Mary)* Come on! There's no future here!

(Exit Mary followed by her mother. Enter Byrne).

BYRNE They've all gone from you now, but maybe that's the way you wanted it.

MAGGIE Maybe. But isn't it natural, Byrne, that the birds should leave the nest when they're fledged. If I left them here they'd turn into four dictators before long.

BYRNE You're hard, Maggie.

MAGGIE I thank God that I am, Byrne! I'm independent now and I'm entitled to be. The hardship of the world will harden my children and they'll have regard for me yet. When I'm gone they're welcome to all I have. No one has a better right to it than they.

BYRNE You'll be lonely.

MAGGIE Anything is better than playing second fiddle to a daughter-in-law. What kind of a life would that be for a woman of my spirit. What I hold God nor man can't take from me. Everyone must make their own nest and by the Lord God the devil's own amount of sweat and blood went into the making of mine.

BYRNE I can't say you're right and I can't say you're wrong.

MAGGIE Ask any woman that signed over what she gave her life to and there's not one that won't agree with Maggie Polpin. When you're down, Byrne, no one will give you a hand-up. I was down long enough but I'm up now and if I'm alone itself I'm my own mistress. I'll get a young girl to help, one that will do what she's told.

BYRNE *(down and out)* You won't consider my offer then?

MAGGIE I'll spend the rest of my life getting the taste of marriage out of my mouth.

BYRNE I have no business around here so. *(goes to exit, is about to leave)*.

MAGGIE Don't say that! You were always welcome in the shop and you always will be welcome in the shop. *(Exit Byrne)*.
(calls after him) While you have the price of the messages in your pocket!

FINAL CURTAIN

MORE PLAYS BY JOHN. B. KEANE

THE MAN FROM CLARE
John B. Keane

The personal tragedy of an aging athlete who finds he no
longer has the physical strength to maintain his position as
captain of the team, and his reputation as the best footballer
in Clare.

THE YEAR OF THE HIKER
John B. Keane

The 'Hiker' is the much hated father who deserted his wife
and family twelve years previously and whose return is awaited
with fear.

THE FIELD
John B. Keane

The Field is a play about the social and moral effects of land
greed. 'A fine play, full of living dialogue, with characters that
come from the author's real understanding of the people, the
problems, and evils of our rural community' — *Standard*.

MOLL
John B. Keane

Hilariously funny, Moll, the comedy by Ireland's most
influential and prolific dramatist, will entertain and amuse
everybody.

VALUES
John B. Keane

In *Values* John B. Keane takes a look at some facets of Irish
life. The first offering *The Spraying of John O'Dorey* takes a
futuristic look at pollution. The comedy is set in a courtroom
in 2052 and the audience laughs at the inanities of ultra-
conservationists. The killing of the avaricious flea can be

acclaimed as a murderous act. John B. Keane smiles at the idea that people may be more expendable than animals. The second play *Blackwater* is a realistic drama which gives value to loneliness, indifference and ingratitude of an only son to his widowed mother. *The Pure of Heart* is a hilarious situation farce taking as its value the moral hypocrisy which places adultery far higher up the ladder of iniquity than cold-blooded murder.

THE CHANGE IN MAME FADDEN
John B. Keane

This powerful drama depicts a woman facing the change of life, and how her family fail to understand the turmoil she is experiencing.

THE CRAZY WALL
John B. Keane

Symbolism is usually the foe of realism in the theatre, but in his latest play John B. Keane has lost none of his realistic force in creating a powerful symbol in the shape of the wall Michael Barnett erects — ostensibly to ward off tramps and other interlopers — but in fact for deeper, intensely personal reasons known only to himself.